BRIAN MILLAWAY

Broken I am not

A learning lesson from growing up LGBT

Contents

1

Chapter 1

Introduction

Thank you and welcome to my book. My name is Brian and I am excited and truth be told, a little nervous about sharing my experience and struggles growing up as a gay man. The purpose of me writing this book is to provide knowledge and educate people who may not know much about the LGBT community. To help people who may be lost and confused or not sure where to turn or who to turn to for help. This was my scenario as you will soon read about. They may know someone LGBT or be LGBT themselves and are looking for answers. Whatever the scenario, I hope the information in this book will provide knowledge and answers to those questions. Unfortunately, some LGBT people will think they have no other choice but to end their own life which is an extremely sad circumstance. If I am able to help just one person, then writing this book will have been absolutely worth it.

I am more than willing to share my memories, struggles and experiences if that will help others. Even though it will mean for me to come out of my comfort zone. Too often, I see on social media that a LGBT person was either kicked out of the family home, beaten just because the person was LGBT, or worse. I felt like it was time for me to do what I can do and at least share my story and hope that it helps someone else who is LGBT.

Please read this book with an open mind because chances are, you either know a close friend, relative, you are an ally, or you yourself are in the LGBT community. I want to again thank you for purchasing my book and I sincerely hope you learn something and it makes a difference. When I say LGBT I of course mean everyone in the LGBT+ community. Also, this is my very first attempt at writing a book so I apologize if it is not written well. English was not my best subject in school.

2

Chapter 2

Early Memories

In 1979 I was born into an amazing family. I am the youngest of two sisters and one brother. Memories of my young childhood are fairly normal. I was a shy kid and had a hard time initiating conversations with someone new. I love making people laugh! I've been told a few times that I would make a great comedian. I just didn't think I am creative enough to come up with funny material. I come up with funny stuff (well, funny to me) every now and again. I guess that's why I started doing tic tok videos. Oh boy, that was probably too much information. Anyway, back to the task at hand. Growing up I always wanted to be a police officer. I have had relatives in law enforcement and that was the profession I chose at an early age. I think that becoming a police officer helped me come out of my shell and not be so shy. As a matter of fact, my first few months on the job, I was told I "wouldn't make it" as a cop because I was so shy. I definitely was a momma's boy. So, it comes to no surprise that I was extremely terrified when my mother left me at grade school by myself for the first time. In grade school I was extremely shy and did not have very many friends at first. I would eventually gain a couple of friends toward the third and fourth grade era in grade school. It was about this time I remember recognizing that I had same sex attraction. As I learned more about sexuality in school I soon began to realize that same sex attraction was not "normal". It was a taboo subject. It wasn't normal for a boy to like a boy. It was about that time I figured something was wrong with me. I thought I was "broken" and felt I could never tell anyone about it. I did not want anyone to think I was broken or a freak. So from then on, I promised myself I would never tell anyone that I had same sex attraction. In 5th grade, I remember my teacher Mr. Whitaker, talking about AIDS and how awful the disease is and how you can die from it, and How only gay people get it. This was extremely terrifying to me. I remember thinking that's how I was going to die. Remember, this is in 1989 so there was no internet for me to do any research. I also could not ask anyone because I did not want anyone to know my secret. So I was stuck with this "demon" in me with no one I could talk to about it. Over the next few years I tried to ignore my same sex attraction feelings. Focusing on other things like having fun, playing sports, and being with friends, as kids do. I played all kinds of sports and loved every minute of it. Baseball was my absolute favorite sport to play. I played every chance I could and I was good at it. I played baseball up until high school and I quit playing. Having all these negative feelings about being broken, made me believe I was not good enough to continue playing baseball. Not only in sports but other things in my life made me feel like I wasn't good or smart enough. My mental health was starting to affect me negatively.

3

Chapter 3

In denial

As I entered high school I still was determined to keep my promise to myself to never tell anyone about my same sex attraction. I told myself that this was a phase and it would go away. I kept telling myself I was not gay over and over again. Too often I would have feelings that I was damaged, that I was broken, or I was a freak. I did not know anyone else who had these feelings that I did. So I was alone in this extremely scary situation. I did not have many friends during high school. My best friends I had during grade school, I had lost. I only had 2 or 3 friends who I would hang out with during lunch time. I hardly ever went to dances. The only dances I went to were the girls' choice dances. I didn't even go to my senior prom. I never had any girlfriends. As a matter of fact I didn't even kiss a girl until after I graduated high school.

At age 14 my parents had me attending church. As the years went by my church strongly preached that homosexuality was a sin. They preached that males must marry a female. The church quite often preached this which made me feel even worse. The more reason I had to keep this secret of mine hidden. I received a little relief when I graduated from high school, one less thing I had to worry about. In 2001 I attended the police academy as it was my lifelong goal to help people being a police officer. I graduated from the academy the next year and started working as a police officer.

As the church taught, when you marry a girl, everything will be okay. As long as you follow God's plan, you will be saved, and you will go to the highest kingdom in heaven. This is what the church taught. So, I started dating girls thinking maybe the church was right. Maybe if I get a girlfriend, my same sex attraction will go away.

As the years went by I dated girls here and there until I met an amazing girl named Stephanie. At the age of 28 Stephanie and I were married.

I was determined to have a normal life and forget all these negative feelings I had for myself. After all, I was just following what I was taught in church. I wanted to be a good guy and go to heaven. I chose to be a police officer so I could help to do good. In movies I always loved when the good guys win. Even in video games I can't be evil if the game gives you the choice, I always chose good.

A year after getting married we had a wonderful son, Dylan. A few years later Dylan ended up getting a diagnosis of severely autisitic. As much as I love him, it is very difficult to raise a child who is severely autistic. The stress still sets in to this day as Dylan continues to struggle with self destructive behaviors. He is still non-verbal at the age of 14 years old. It was normal for him to go to sleep at 11:00 pm or midnight and be up for the day at 2:00 or 3:00 am. Needless to say, this rapidly took a toll on, not only my own mental health but Stephanie's as well. Depression and severe anxiety soon set in. It took our state a couple of years (which felt like an eternity) to finally realize Dylan desperately needs medicaid so he can receive the therapy he needs.

Working a stressful job as a police officer with rotating shifts, having a severely autistic child, and still denying myself that I have same sex attraction, took its toll and I began having suicidal thoughts. There were countless nights I was staring at my firearm and thinking I could have relief with just one pull of the trigger. I even held my firearm and pointed it to my head one difficult night. As I was debating whether or not to pull the trigger, the thought of how much Dylan needs me entered my mind. So I lowered my firearm willing to fight another day.

I still had the feeling that I could not speak to anyone about me having same sex attraction. I mean, I couldn't. I'm supposed to be manly, which was another reason why I did not seek out professional help. After all, who ever heard of a gay cop. I would be shunned, hated, and perhaps fired.

One night I thought if I were to write my feelings down, perhaps it would help. So I went onto my computer and started to type my feelings about same sex attraction. I typed everything about why I was so depressed and anxious starting from my childhood. When I finished typing I saved it and kept it pretty well hidden on the computer, or so I thought. As time went on I would occasionally open up that letter and add to it if I was feeling depressed.

4

Chapter 4

Self Acceptance

At some point a light bulb went off and I asked myself a few questions. "Why the hell am I fighting myself on this?" "Why am I still denying the fact that I have same sex attraction?" "What will happen if I just accept the fact that I am attracted to guys?" I thought how exhausting it is to my mental health for me to keep fighting and denying myself the fact that I have same sex attraction. So, at that point I accept it. I finally accepted myself for who I am. This was the first step for me to actually get some relief regarding my secret. However, there was a new wave of depression setting in. I've accepted myself for who I am, that's great and all but, I still cannot let out my secret. After all, I am married and it would for sure end in divorce. I felt I had no choice but to keep being married at the cost of my own mental health.

As time went on I still had bouts of depression, anxiety and occasional suicide ideation. Some days were better than others. One day I received a text message from Stephanie that struck me as odd. The message simply asked if I was okay. I responded that I was and asked her what made her think that I wasn't okay. Before I tell you her response. Let me ask you a question. Remember when I said I thought I hid the letter I was writing deep within the computer? Well, apparently not. She said she found this letter on the computer and was worried. I did mention in the letter that I have suicidal ideation. I assured her I was fine and we would discuss it when I returned home from the funeral I was attending. My heart sank. The cat was out of the bag. What have I done? I had so many emotions running through me I couldn't even think.

5

Chapter 5

Coming out

When I returned home we had our discussion about the letter. I was very surprised and extremely grateful for how supportive Stephanie was. I was expecting a very difficult discussion but it turned out to be very pleasant. She told me she would not say anything and would allow me to tell my family when I was ready, and for that I'm extremely grateful. I was a little more relieved knowing that someone else knew, although it wasn't the ideal situation in the way she found out. But regardless, another person knew I have an attraction to the same sex. This was the second step of getting relief from my secret. We stayed married for a year or so (I can't remember exactly how long) later before getting a devorce. I felt absolutely horrible even though the divorce was mutual. Feeling like a horrible person, still feeling broken, and all those other negative feelings, I decided to seek professional help from a therapist.

Therapy helped me immensely! I learned that I'm not broken and I'm definitely not the only person who had the same issues. As a matter of fact, I learned it is common. I continued to go to therapy for quite some time. At this point two people knew I was gay. I knew I had to tell my family and friends at some point but was extremely terrified of the thought. I was going through multiple scenarios in my head, the worst being that my family would disown me. My friends would hate me and my coworkers would never speak to me again. I had to think of a way to tell my family but was just not ready. However, I did have an idea on how to do it. Right after Christmas each year my parents would go to their summer home in Arizona and stay there until April or so. Having the belief that time heals wounds, I had the thought of mailing the letter to my parents summer home and perhaps they wouldn't disown me when they return in a few months. They could also tell the rest of my family so I didn't have to. I felt like this was the best option for me.

The day after Christmas in 2018, I printed out the letter. The letter that explains how I like guys and have had those feelings since grade school. The letter I had saved on my computer all these years. I placed it in an envelope, addressed it, and slapped a stamp on it, and without thinking about it, I threw it in the mailbox with no chance of getting it back. A wave of relief and anxiety hit me at the same time. In a short few days my parents would know my secret. This was approximately a year after the divorce. Before I show you a copy of it, be advised that I did make a little change. I changed the journal style letter that I was adding and deleting from to an actual letter form, but still keeping it genuine. Oh, and forgive any spelling or grammar errors in it as well, I wanted to keep it genuine. So with that, here is a copy of the letter I sent to my family:

My Dear Family,

There has been something that has been living inside me for decades. Something that I have been too terrified to talk about. I still am terrified at this very moment at what I am about to tell you. There are tones of emotions I am experiencing including fear and relief. If, when you are done reading this, you do not want anything to do with me I will understand. But what I am asking for is understanding and acceptance. I cannot handle anything negative at this point and I hope after reading this you will understand why.

This thing is most terrifying for me to reveal, but it's time. At a very young age I started to receive certain feelings. Feelings of attraction to the same sex. I denied those feelings. Telling myself that these "wrong" feelings will go away. They didn't. I kept in denial for years and years but these feelings would not go away. I kept asking myself what was wrong with me? "am I broken"? "am I a freak"? I have cried myself to sleep wondering what is wrong with me. I have even had countless nights contemplating suicide. I have even held my gun up to my head wanting to end it all. I wanted to die. I wanted to end this miserable life. I hated it. I hate this life. I hated all these feelings. I can't be gay, I just cant be. Terrified to say anything, and because it was drilled in my head that homosexuality is wrong by the church, I also kept this secret. I promised myself that I would never tell anyone. But that started to take a toll on me, feeling depressed and suicidal. Looking back I should have sought out help earlier. But again I was terrified about what people would think of me.

Still denying these feelings, I got married thinking everything will be ok, that these feelings will go away, but they didn't. Besides, that's what the church wants you to do and everything will be fine, right? To get married to a woman? (this is not the reason we got divorced by the way) These feelings for guys still did not go away. I started to get extremely exhausted mentally, physically and emotionally that I finally accepted my feelings. I finally accepted that I was attracted to guys. This took a toll on me keeping this secret all these years. After receiving therapy I realized that nothing is "wrong" with me and it felt good to get these things off my chest. Now I just need to get the monkey off my shoulders, which is what I'm doing now. Therapy has helped. Been going for a year and a half and I realized I'm not the only one in this situation. I needed to get this out for my own sake and my mental health.

I understand the strong church culture surrounding this state. Them drilling into everyone's head that homosexuality is wrong and it is of the worst sin anyone can commit. That's one of the reasons why I told myself that I would never tell anyone. But, not telling anyone just about killed me. Literally, mentally and emotionally. I see things differently than the church. I'm a good guy. I'm not a monster. I'm not a pedophile. I'm not some sexually crazed person. I'm still the same old person just like before. I fight for good in my profession. If god wants to send a good person to hell just because he is attracted to the same sex, then so be it. For that is the only "crime" I have committed and will commit in this life. You have your own beliefs and I respect that. The only thing I ask for is acceptance. You don't have to agree, I only ask you to accept me and continue with life just as before.

Something that I have done is compare myself to criminals I see at work. Thinking things like "at least I've never hurt or killed anyone" or "at least I don't steal things", Or "at least I don't do drugs and am in and out of jail all the time and can't be there for my son". Just trying to justify to myself that I am a good guy. Things are better now. Sure, I still have bad days and have some depression and anxiety but it has been better than the past. Therapy has helped. I have accepted who I am and hope you will do the same. Steph and I are still great friends. She has actually been my biggest support. Well, my only support truth be told, (at the current time) but she has been great.

I have felt alone the last 2 years or so but I have also confided in a couple friends who are gay and they have offered me support. As I have stated before I have been seeing a therapist. I have confided all of this to him and I believe it has given me more courage everyday. I have made 2018 the year where I tried to learn new skills. I have become a physical trainer and I made a goal to learn Spanish (a very long work in progress). I am definitely not done learning. I am continuing my quest to learn Spanish, I won't give up until I can be conversational. I know the most Spanish I have ever known before and want to learn more. That's just a personal goal I have always wanted to accomplish. It may take me a while but I will get there. There are also some promotional opportunities at work that I will put in for, so we will see what happens there. Perhaps I'm trying to better myself to justify the way I am. Whatever the reason, I have been very ambitious the last 2 or so years.

Well, there it is. You can hate me, disown me, support me, or never speak to me again. Whatever you choose I will still be the same old person. I am hoping and asking for support. I am going through a little tough time right now until this is all over. But with the help of my therapist I am able to get by. I hope I have answered all your questions because I will be a nervous wreck when I send these out and won't be ready to answer a bunch of questions for a long time. I am going to ask you to please don't contact me for a while unless it is for support. Thank you for your understanding. I love you all.

Your Son and Brother,

Brian

By the way, learning Spanish is still very much a work in progress. I need to get that ambitious drive I had before and start working towards my goal of being conversational.

6

Chapter 6

Relationship with family after coming out

Aweek went by and I had not heard anything. Surely they had received the letter by now. I was only one state away. Every time my phone beeped or vibrated was extremely nerve racking for me. A couple of weeks after I sent the letter I received a phone call from my older brother. Before I tell you what happened in the phone call, let me give you some background. I am the youngest of four kids. From oldest to youngest is my sister Sheri, god rest her soul. Then my older brother Mike, and then my sister Brooke. I love my siblings dearly! With all the scenarios that ran through my head I thought my brother would be the one to be the harshest on me. A few years ago when the gay marrige law began to legalize, I noticed some posts on facebook he made to voice his displeasure about the situation. When I saw that post I for sure thought he would be the one who would disown me first.

Now back to the phone call I got from my brother. I answered the call and my brother said he fully supported me and that he was deeply sorry for everything I had to go through. That was truly a breath of fresh air to hear. My brother also assured me that I definitely have the support of my other sisters. This was truly a huge weight lifted off my shoulders. I can't recall how long I cried after that phone call. I feel like my brother and I are even closer now than before I came out. A couple days later I received a phone call from my dad. I remember because I was actually on a date with a guy. The basics of the phone call from my dad were, my parents are supportive but conflicted. I took that as a win. I did not want to explain anything further at that time. I told him thank you for supporting me. I told him I loved him and mom, and that was the short phone call from my dad. That was a huge step, the biggest step of all and I finally had relief knowing my family was aware and that I had their support.

However, I wasn't out of the woods yet. A few months later I made a decision to write up a Facebook post and post that I was coming out. I wanted to let everyone know at once so I didn't have to make an explanation over and over again. Right after I made the post, I logged out of Facebook because I was extremely nervous about what people were going to say. A couple days later I mustered up the courage to log back in. I was greeted with overwhelming support. I read every comment on my post and I don't recall anything negative. For me, that was the final step. I have no words to express how appreciative I was from everyone's support.

7

Chapter 7

My advice

I would like to add this short chapter and express some of the things I wish I had done. The first thing I wished I had done was sought help sooner. Please please please seek out help if you are struggling like I did. Talk to anyone! A school counselor, a trusted clergy member, a friend, a therapist, call a crisis hotline. I promise you are not the first one to seek help about being LGBT. When I spoke to my therapist, it really helped me! I still continue to see my therapist when times get tough. I am extremely lucky I did not follow through on what I wanted to do on those dark nights. I was literally an inch from death. It absolutely breaks my heart when I hear about an LGBT person taking their own life because they felt like they had no other option.

Coming out can be an extremely scary experience. There is no time limit. The time is right when you are ready. I was 39 years old when I came out as gay.

Try to have thick skin. There are people who hate us and that is sad but a reality. People will say some things that will be hurtful. Try not to let those words hurt you. Sadly there are mean people who just like to be mean. Please try your hardest not to get offended and ignore these people. I do understand it is easier said than done, however. Being in law enforcement for 19 years (only one more year until I can retire from it, thank the lord above!) I've been called every name in the book so it takes a lot for me to get offended. Besides, I am a nice guy so why would you try. Haha.

Parents, if your son or daughter comes out as LGBT please don't shut them out. Continue to love them as your child. It saddens me when I hear of a child being kicked out, disowned or shunned by their own parents. It's okay to not agree with it but please be supportive at the very least.

Get involved! There are countless LGBT groups! An example of a group that I'm involved in and love is Stonewall Sports. It's an LGBT group that provides kickball, volleyball, dodgeball and many more sports for people to play. Don't worry, you don't have to be an athlete to play. I strongly encourage you to research any LGBT groups available in your area. There are also endless social media LGBT groups as well. Just be cautious as social media can make you feel unsafe.

8

Chapter 8

Facts and myths

I wanted to add this quick section to hopefully help people understand or get some clarification on some common stereotypes. These are my own feelings and opinions as I have experienced them, I do not want to speak for everyone who is LGBT.

Myth: Being gay is a choice.

Fact: I don't know how I could have made that choice at such a young age. I was so confused and conflicted about having same sex attraction. I was more concerned about people possibly finding out, so I kept it hidden. I also wouldn't subject myself to all the depression, anxiety and suicidal ideation just for choosing to be gay. I feel like I had as much choice to be gay as my son Dylan did being severly autistic.

Myth: Gay men can choose to be straight.

Fact: Well, I sure did not work for me. Again, I would have just switched straight then to have gone through all that torment I went through.

Myth: Gay men are pedophiles.

Fact: This is a disturbing one and I hate it. Although there probably are gay pedophiles as well as straight pedophiles, both are extreamly wrong and I get absolutely disgusted and furious about this stereotype.

Myth: Gay men die of AIDS eventually.

Fact: Although AIDS is still a valid concern, there are way more safeguard and treatment options available nowadays. An example is the prescription Prep, and when taken correctly, can be very effective in preventing HIV.

Chapter 9

Resources

There are several resources available if you need immediate help, have questions or just need to speak to someone. Please utilize these resources! The second link has a whole list of resources for people in different situations.

Trevor Project. (n.d.). *The Trevor Project*. Retrieved July 29, 2022, from http://trevorproject.org/get-help-now/

Glaad. (n.d.). *LGBTQ resource list*. Retrieved July 30, 2022, from https://www.glaad.org/resourcelist
Sage. (n.d.). *Sage*. Retrieved July 30, 2022, from https://www.sageusa.org/what-we-do/sage-national-lgbt-elder-hotline/

10

Chapter 10

Conclusion

I want to personally thank you for your time and your willingness to read my book. As you may have already gathered, I really am passionate about the LGBT community. As I mentioned before, the main reason why I wrote this book was to help other people who are LGBT. I genuinely hope that you learned a thing or two. I hope it was informative and interesting. Not that I'm a famous person or writer or anything. I'm nobody special. I'm just a person who felt like my experiences and the information in this book may possibly help someone else, and that was the main goal! Again, thank you so much and God Bless!

If you found this book enjoyable or helpful I would really appreciate a favorable review for it on Amazon! Thank you very much!